GREAT FILM SONGS

LONDON / NEW YORK / MADRID / TOKYO

D1419771

ALSO AVAILABLE IN THE *REALLY EASY PIANO* SERIES...

ABBA
25 GREAT HITS. ORDER NO. AM980430

BALLADS
24 CHART POP HITS. ORDER NO. AM982751

THE BEATLES
23 BEATLES HITS. ORDER NO. NO91080

CHART HITS
21 BIG CHART HITS. ORDER NO. AM993377

CHRISTMAS
24 FESTIVE CHART HITS. ORDER NO. AM980496

CLASSICAL
36 POPULAR PIECES. ORDER NO. AM980419

ELTON JOHN
24 CLASSIC SONGS. ORDER NO. AM987844

FILM SONGS
24 SCREEN HITS. ORDER NO. AM980441

FRANK SINATRA
21 POPULAR SONGS ORDER NO. AM987833

JAZZ
24 JAZZ CLASSICS. ORDER NO. AM982773

POP HITS
22 GREAT SONGS. ORDER NO. AM980408

SHOWSTOPPERS
24 STAGE HITS. ORDER NO. AM982784

TV HITS
25 POPULAR HITS. ORDER NO. AM985435

60s HITS
25 CLASSIC HITS. ORDER NO. AM985402

70s HITS
25 CLASSIC SONGS. ORDER NO. AM985413

80s HITS
25 POPULAR HITS. ORDER NO. AM985424

90s HITS
24 POPULAR HITS. ORDER NO. AM987811

50 POPULAR SONGS
FROM POP SONGS TO CLASSICAL THEMES. ORDER NO. AM994400

21st CENTURY HITS
24 POPULAR HITS. ORDER NO. AM987822

ALL TITLES CONTAIN BACKGROUND NOTES FOR EACH SONG PLUS
PLAYING TIPS AND HINTS.

PUBLISHED BY
WISE PUBLICATIONS
14-15 BERNERS STREET, LONDON, W1T 3LJ, UK.

EXCLUSIVE DISTRIBUTORS:
MUSIC SALES LIMITED
DISTRIBUTION CENTRE, NEWMARKET ROAD, BURY ST EDMUNDS,
SUFFOLK, IP33 3YB, UK.
MUSIC SALES PTY LIMITED
20 RESOLUTION DRIVE, CARINGBAH, NSW 2229, AUSTRALIA.

ORDER NO. AM993344
ISBN 978-1-84772-529-5
THIS BOOK © COPYRIGHT 2008 BY WISE PUBLICATIONS,
A DIVISION OF MUSIC SALES LIMITED.

MUSIC ARRANGED BY ZOE BOLTON.
MUSIC PROCESSED BY PAUL EWERS MUSIC DESIGN.
EDITED BY FIONA BOLTON.
PRINTED IN THE EU.

YOUR GUARANTEE OF QUALITY
AS PUBLISHERS, WE STRIVE TO PRODUCE EVERY BOOK TO THE HIGHEST
COMMERCIAL STANDARDS. THE MUSIC HAS BEEN FRESHLY ENGRAVED AND
THE BOOK HAS BEEN CAREFULLY DESIGNED TO MINIMISE AWKWARD PAGE
TURNS AND TO MAKE PLAYING FROM IT A REAL PLEASURE.
PARTICULAR CARE HAS BEEN GIVEN TO SPECIFYING ACID-FREE, NEUTRAL-
SIZED PAPER MADE FROM PULPS WHICH HAVE NOT BEEN ELEMENTAL
CHLORINE BLEACHED. THIS PULP IS FROM FARMED SUSTAINABLE FORESTS
AND WAS PRODUCED WITH SPECIAL REGARD FOR THE ENVIRONMENT.
THROUGHOUT, THE PRINTING AND BINDING HAVE BEEN PLANNED TO
ENSURE A STURDY, ATTRACTIVE PUBLICATION WHICH SHOULD GIVE YEARS
OF ENJOYMENT. IF YOUR COPY FAILS TO MEET OUR HIGH STANDARDS,
PLEASE INFORM US AND WE WILL GLADLY REPLACE IT.

WWW.MUSICSALES.COM

Breaking Free

Words & Music by Jamie Houston

This track, from the phenomenally successful Disney movie, recorded the fastest ever climb in Billboard Hot 100 history and was one of five songs from the film to feature simultaneously. Zac Efron also became the first artist to debut with two songs in the same week although the voice in the movie itself is that of Drew Seeley!

Hints & Tips: The chorus (bars 21–36) should be played with more energy than the rest of the song. Keep the L.H. light and bouncy and make sure the tempo doesn't drag when you get to the tricky corners in the R.H. (bars 23–24 and 31–32).

-ing free. Oh, we're break - ing free. We're run - ning,

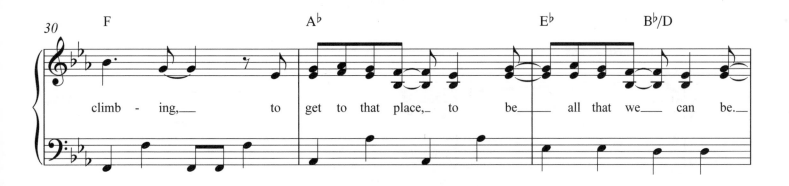

climb - ing, to get to that place, to be all that we can be.

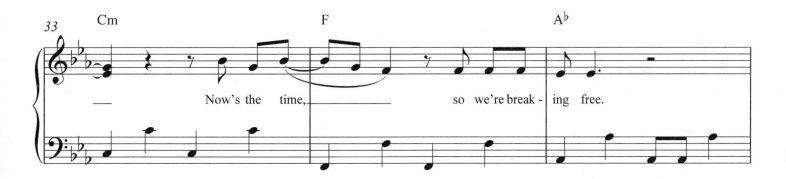

Now's the time, so we're break - ing free.

Oh. We know the world can see us

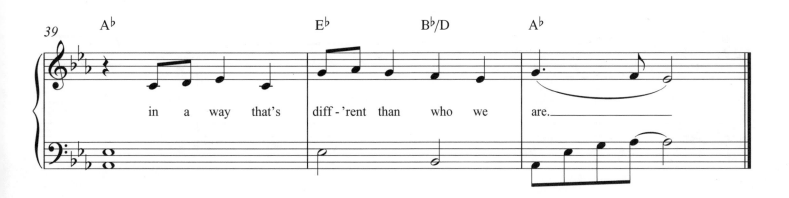

in a way that's diff -'rent than who we are.

Angel

Words & Music by Sarah McLachlan

Originally from the 1997 album *Surfacing*, this track is often used to highlight emotional scenes in films and TV shows. In *City Of Angels* Nicolas Cage plays Seth, an angel who appears to those who are dying or about to die.

Hints & Tips: Play this piece as smoothly (legato) as possible, holding each note for its full length. Where the same note is repeated, think about which is the most important in the phrase and play it with slightly more weight.

Blue Velvet

Words & Music by Bernie Wayne & Lee Morris

The soundtrack to this film features vintage pop songs juxtaposed with an orchestral score inspired by Shostakovich, in particular his Symphony No. 15. Despite only moderate box office success, this mystery/thriller opened to widespread critical acclaim and has since become a cult classic.

Hints & Tips: Watch out for the accidentals in bars 17–24 and remember that a sharp or flat symbol only applies from the point it appears until the end of that bar. Some cautionary accidentals have been printed to assist you.

Born Free

Words by Don Black. Music by John Barry

Along with lyricist Don Black, composer John Barry won the 1966 Oscar for Best Original Song for this track and another, Best Original Music Score, for his soundtrack to the film. Based on the best-selling book by Joy Adamson, the film narrates how she and her game warden husband George raise Elsa, an orphaned lion cub.

Hints & Tips: Pratise the L.H. until you are comfortable and confident with the repetitive rhythmic pattern. Then add the R.H. but keep to a steady pace, using a metronome to regulate the tempo if required.

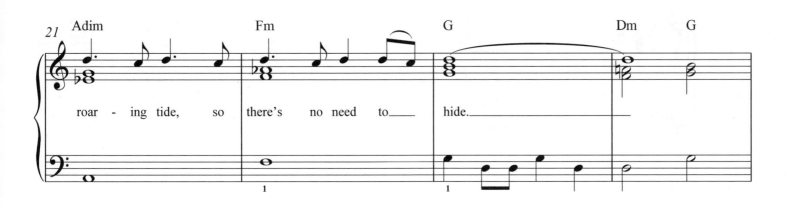

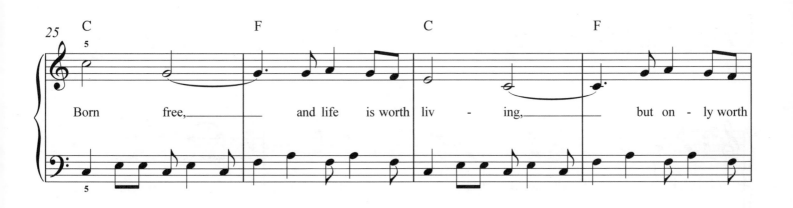

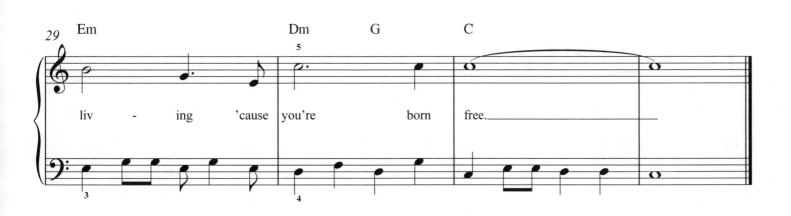

Can't Fight The Moonlight

Words & Music by Diane Warren

This is one of four songs performed by country star LeAnn Rimes for the character Violet, a would-be songwriter who goes to New York to pursue her dreams and gets a job as a barmaid at the Coyote Ugly Saloon. Rimes has a cameo role in the film, effectively duetting with herself!

Hints & Tips: Don't be put off by the fact that the words you would naturally emphasise often fall on the weak beats of the bar, rather than the strong beats as you would usually expect. Playing it slowly at first might help you keep your wits about you.

Diamonds Are A Girl's Best Friend

Words by Leo Robin. Music by Jule Styne

First sung by Carol Channing in a 1949 Broadway production, in the role of Lorelei Lee, a blonde, naïve, dim-witted, but gorgeous showgirl hussy, Marilyn Monroe's performance of this song, descending a staircase, has been copied by more modern icons such as Madonna, Kylie Minogue, Anna Nicole Smith and Nicole Kidman.

Hints & Tips: Create a marked contrast between the march-like opening and the bouncy remainder of this piece by adhering to the tempo change and playing the second half with a much lighter touch.

Everybody's Talkin'

Words & Words & Music by Fred Neil

Nilsson won the 1969 Grammy for Best Male Pop Vocal Performance for this track from the soundtrack of a movie which charts the unlikely companionship and tragic drama of two homeless down-and-out drifters, played by Dustin Hoffman and Jon Voight, the first and only X-rated film to be awarded an Oscar for Best Picture.

Hints & Tips: Between the melodic phrases are snippets of accompaniment (notes without words underneath). Keep these light so that there is a distinction between the melody and accompaniment.

Hallelujah

Words & Music by Leonard Cohen

First recorded, with 15 verses, by Leonard Cohen on his 1984 album *Various Positions*, and nominated by *Q Magazine* in September 2007 as the most perfect song ever, various versions of this song have featured on the soundtracks of several movies and TV shows, most often during scenes which involve death or heartbreak.

Hints & Tips: Pay careful attention to placing the R.H. and L.H. notes together, especially the last quaver beat of each bar.

I Believe I Can Fly

Words & Music by R. Kelly

This Grammy Award-winning song has become popular at high school graduations, and an inspirational anthem at weddings and in video tributes since featuring in the 1996 film which mixes live action and animation, starring Bugs Bunny and other *Looney Tunes* characters opposite professional basketball star Michael Jordan.

Hints & Tips: Start this piece quite softly and use a crescendo (getting louder) through bars 9–12 to build intensity as you approach the chorus. This will create a contrast between the melancholy verse and the positive climax of the chorus.

I Don't Want To Miss A Thing

Words & Music by Diane Warren

Originally intended for Celine Dion, this love theme from the sci-fi movie in which a group of deep core drillers is sent by NASA to deflect an asteroid on a collision course with earth, became Aerosmith's first No. 1 hit on the Billboard Top 100 after 28 years together, and earned them an Academy Award nomination for Best Song.

Hints & Tips: You will find that your R.H. has to move around quite a lot and make a few stretches in this piece. Make life easier for yourself by keeping the tempo reasonably slow and not rushing through the semiquavers.

I Walk The Line

Words & Music by Johnny Cash

The chronicle of the life of country music legend Johnny Cash, from his upbringing on an Arkansas cotton farm to a recording career with Sun Records in Memphis, took its title from his first No. 1 hit, which featured the 'freight train' rhythm common to many of his songs and, in its original form, a key change between every verse.

Hints & Tips: Note that the tempo indication uses a minim rather than a crotchet because this song should have a strong feeling of 'in two' rather than 'in four'. Why not try playing through the piece more than once, perhaps with contrasting dynamics?

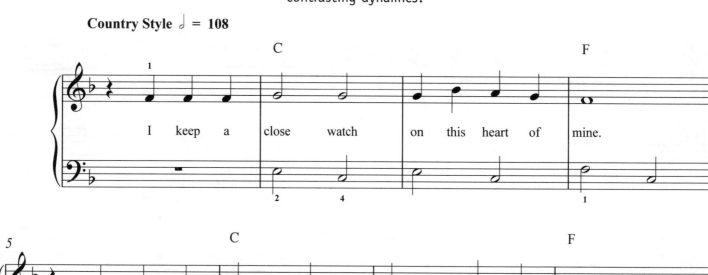

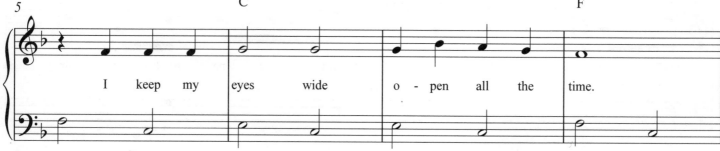

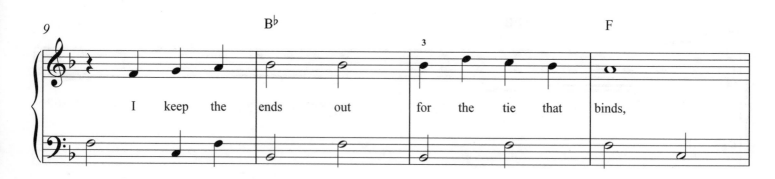

Nine To Five

Words & Music by Dolly Parton

With the clacking of a typewriter in the background, this Grammy Award-winning song and US No. 1 hit features on the soundtrack of the 1980 comedy in which three female employees set out to get even with their odious, sexist boss. Making her film debut, Dolly Parton stars alongside Jane Fonda and Lily Tomlin.

Hints & Tips: Keep your wrists loose in the first eight bars to enable you to maintain a light, bouncy feel to the repeated quavers and semiquavers.

nine to five.___ What a way to make a liv - ing. Bare - ly

get - ting by, it's all tak - ing and no giv - ing. They just

use___ your mind and you nev - er get the cre - dit. It's e -

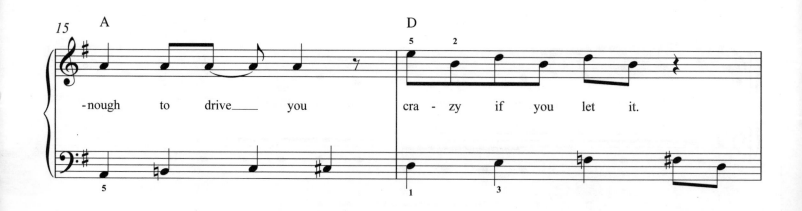

-nough to drive___ you cra - zy if you let it.

Nine to five.____ For____ ser - vice and de - vo - tion, you would

think____ that I would de - serve a fair pro - mo - tion. Want to

move____ a - head, but the boss won't seem to let me. I

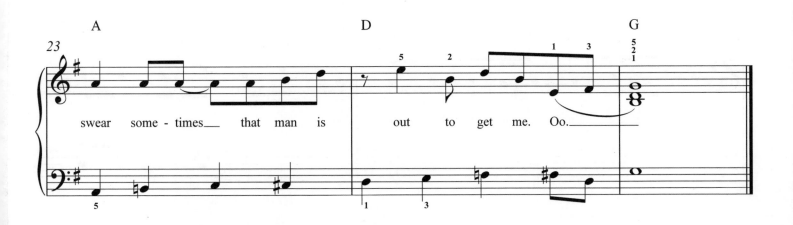

swear some - times____ that man is out to get me. Oo.____

27

Knockin' On Heaven's Door

Words & Music by Bob Dylan

When released by Bob Dylan in 1973, featuring primarily instrumental music, the soundtrack to this Sam Peckinpah film was given a lukewarm reception. However this song became a big hit, and even more so in 1996 when a new version was recorded in memory of the schoolchildren and teacher killed in the Dunblane massacre.

Hints & Tips: Practise the R.H. in bars 9–16 slowly, ensuring you are playing the two notes at exactly the same time.

Knock, knock, knock-in' on heav-en's door.

Knock, knock, knock-in' on heav-en's door.

Knock, knock, knock-in' on hea-ven's door.

Knock, knock, knock-in' on heav-en's door.

One Day I'll Fly Away

Words by Will Jennings. Music by Joe Sample

Featuring exuberant music, elaborate sets and intricate costumes, the cinematic musical in which this song features has a storyline and structure inspired by Italian grand opera. Nicole Kidman sings with poignant melancholy and emotion as her character expresses a hopeless longing to be free of the life she is living.

Hints & Tips: Watch out for the many accidentals in this piece, especially after the key changes. Mark in any extra cautionary accidentals you need to help you remember all the sharps and flats.

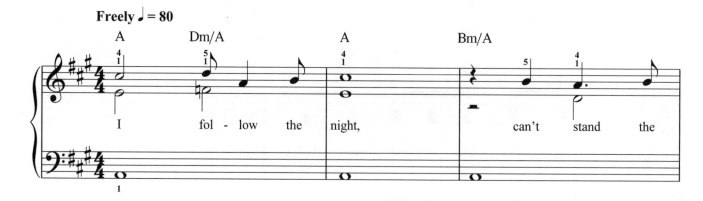

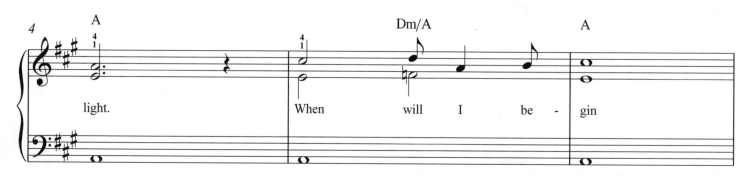

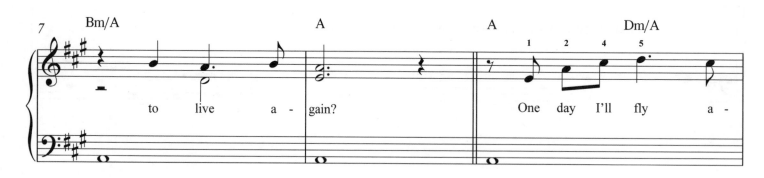

What more could your love do for me, when will love be

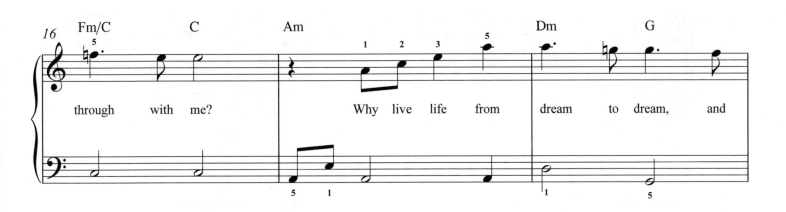

through with me? Why live life from dream to dream, and

dread the day when dream - ing ends.

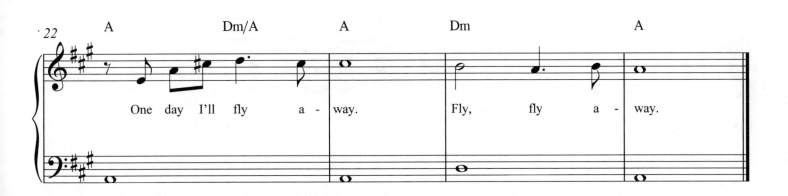

One day I'll fly a - way. Fly, fly a - way.

Pure Shores

Words & Music by Shaznay Lewis & William Orbit

Based on a novel by Alex Garland, *The Beach* stars Leonardo Di Caprio as a young American backpacker who finds a mysterious map in a Bangkok hotel which leads him to a utopian Western settlement. Written for the film, this song, from All Saints' second album *Saints and Sinners*, topped the UK singles charts in February 2000.

Hints & Tips: There is a lot of syncopation in this song, especially in the chorus. Mark in the crotchet beats with a vertical line above the stave if this helps you.

Rule The World

Words & Music by Mark Owen, Gary Barlow, Jason Orange & Howard Donald

Written especially for this fantasy film based on a Neil Gaiman novel and starring Robert De Niro and Michelle Pfeiffer, this song was added to later editions of Take That's 2007 album *Beautiful World*. As a single, despite never reaching No. 1, it became the UK's fifth biggest-seller of the year.

Hints & Tips: Listen carefully to the R.H. in the passage from bar 12 to the end, ensuring that the two notes sound together. Practise this separately if you need to.

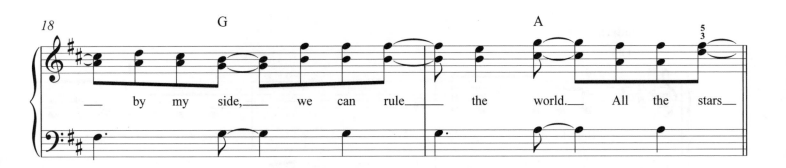

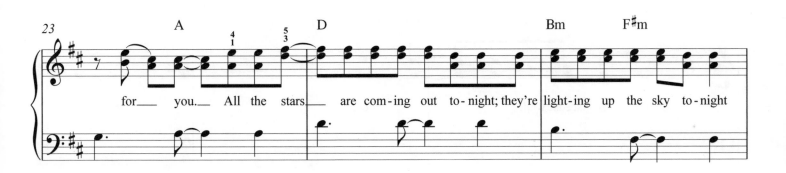

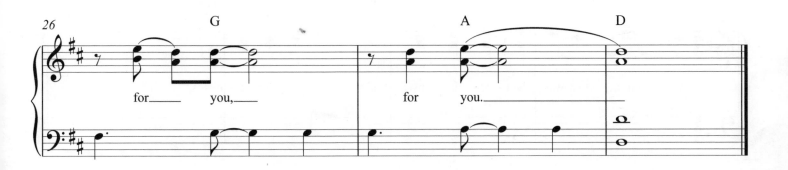

The Sound Of Silence

Words & Music by Paul Simon

First recorded in 1964 as an acoustic track on their first album *Wednesday Morning 3AM*, which was not a commercial success, this only became the duo's first hit after producer Tom Wilson, without their knowledge, overdubbed it with electric instruments, tapping into the folk-rock movement prevalent at the time.

Hints & Tips: Whilst holding the semibreves, look ahead to the next bar. This will help you achieve smooth transitions between the two hands.

Stayin' Alive

Words & Music by Barry Gibb, Maurice Gibb & Robin Gibb

Along with *Night Fever, How Deep Is Your Love, More Than A Woman* and *If I Can't Have You*, this was one of five original songs written and recorded by The Bee Gees for this film about discomania starring John Travolta. When released as a single it was one of four consecutive USA No. 1 hits which Barry Gibb had a hand in writing.

Hints & Tips: A loose R.H. wrist will help you to play bars 9–12 and avoid it sounding heavy.

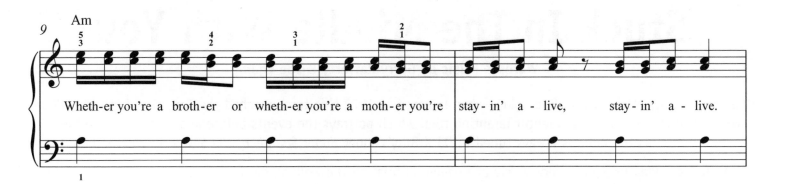

Wheth-er you're a broth-er or wheth-er you're a moth-er you're stay-in' a - live, stay-in' a - live.

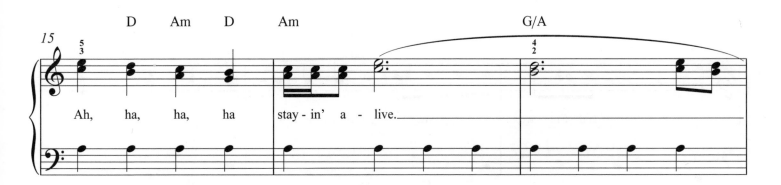

Feel the cit - y break-in' and ev -'ry - bod - y shak - in' and we're stay - in' a - live, stay - in' a - live.

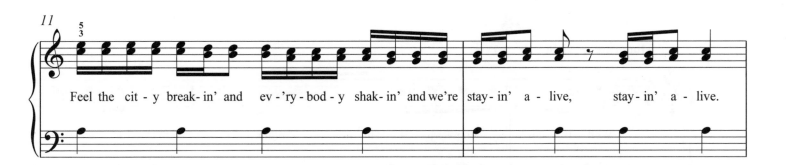

Ah, ha, ha, ha stay - in' a - live, stay - in' a - live.

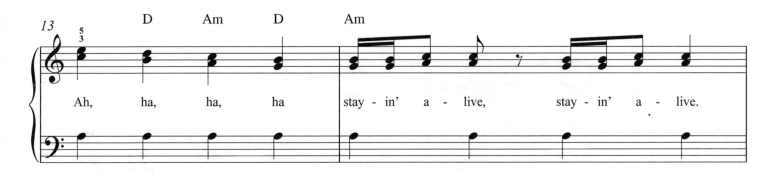

Ah, ha, ha, ha stay - in' a - live.

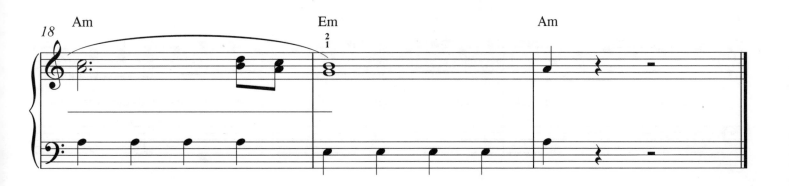

Stuck In The Middle With You
Words & Music by Gerry Rafferty & Joe Egan

Often mistakenly attributed to Bob Dylan, when released in 1972 this track reached the Top 10 in both the UK and US. It features in the 1992 Quentin Tarantino film, which portrays the events before and after a botched jewel heist, as the radio is always tuned to DJ K-Billy's show, *Super Sounds of the Seventies Weekend*.

Hints & Tips: Play this piece very slowly at first, co-ordinating the walking bass of the L.H. and the R.H. melody. It's tricky but definitely not impossible so just take your time!

41

RAY

Unchain My Heart

Words & Music by Bobby Sharp & Teddy Powell

With lyrics begging for release from a one-sided love affair, this track was released as a single by Ray Charles, accompanied by his Raelettes in 1961. It was also the working title for the 2004 biopic starring James Fox in the title role, for which he was won an Oscar for Best Actor. Sadly, Ray Charles died just before the film opened.

Hints & Tips: Practise the L.H. riff alone at first and only add the R.H. melody over the top when you have got the hang of the funky beat.

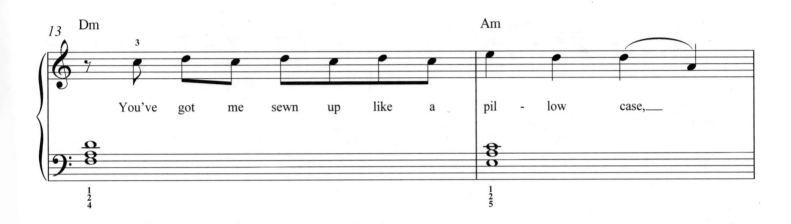

You've Got A Friend In Me

Words & Music by Randy Newman

Since the 1980s, Randy Newman has worked mainly as a film composer, his work on *Toy Story* establishing his trademark animation sound, subsequently carried over to several other scores for Pixar films. Nominated for an Oscar for this song, Newman finally won such an award in 2002 after no fewer than 15 unfruitful nominations.

Hints & Tips: Play this piece with a gentle swing to capture the laid-back feel of the song, but don't become too relaxed—there are plenty of accidentals to keep an eye out for!

You Know My Name

Words & Music by David Arnold & Chris Cornell

Unusually for a James Bond theme, this track doesn't mention the film title in its lyrics, although they do make reference to casino gambling. Chris Cornell is the first American male artist to perform such a theme song and he cites as his inspiration Paul McCartney's theme for *Live And Let Die* and that of Tom Jones for *Thunderball*.

Hints & Tips: The persistent quavers in the L.H. will tire you out unless you keep a loose wrist. Placing an emphasis on the first beat of each bar will also give you a sense of direction. If it's still too much, play crotchets instead of quavers but try to retain the intensity.